Buddhism

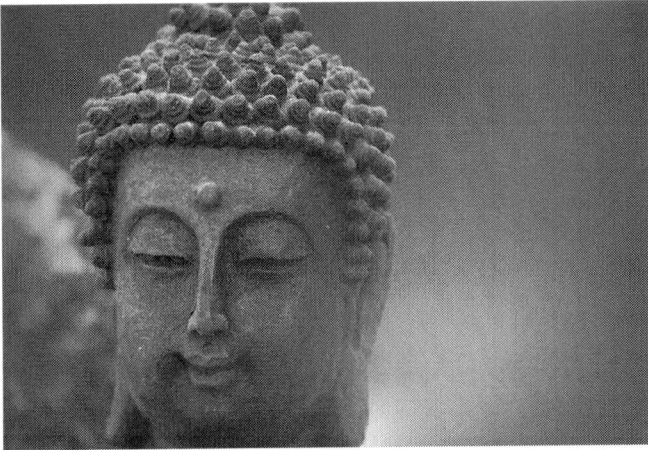

50 Buddhist Teachings for Happiness,
Spiritual Healing, and Enlightenment

By John Baskin

John Baskin

as a result of the use of information contained within this document, including, but not limited to, —errors, omissions, or inaccuracies.

Discretion: I am just a passionate student of health & wellness and am looking for the most cutting edge strategies that can benefit my life, which inspires me to share this knowledge to anyone willing to listen.

Author's Note: I realize that my words will not resonate with every reader. As a man committed to constant and never-ending improvement, if you have any <u>constructive feedback</u> that you would like to offer, or feel like the content in my book can be <u>improved</u> in any way...

...please feel free to contact me at:

<u>faithinknowledge@bookenthuziast.com</u>

Money-back Guarantee: If you are not satisfied with the content inside my books for any reason, you can also get a refund within 7 days of purchase. Simply hover over *Your Account* and click on *Manage Your Content and Device*. Then select the *Action* button directly next to the book you'd like a refund for, and click on *Return for refund*.

Final Note: I am fine with people wanting refunds and, if so, I would still appreciate if you'd be kind enough to contact me via email regarding your opinion and ways you believe I can improve my book. That would be extremely helpful ☺

Table of Contents

John Baskin

Teaching 1:   The Basic Tenets of Buddhism as a Way of Life

"No one saves us but ourselves. No one can and no one may.

We ourselves must walk the path." - Siddhartha

At first glance, and from the perspective of an outsider, Buddhism may be thought of as a far-fetched belief practiced by monks in robes, holding incense. It is a religion that seems unattached to the real world. At first glance, it may even appear similar to a devotion that only highly spiritual people will be able to practice.

Looking closer, you will see that there is more to it than is popularly believed to be the picture of this so-called religion. Spectators interested in understanding the more about Buddhism will realize that Buddhism promotes nothing less than cultivation of the mind. It is not at all a religious obligation, but a life-long commitment to an ethical way of living.

Firstly, it is important to understand that Buddha was not a God. He was not the creator of beings, or a superhuman who made miracles happen. He was a mortal, a man who is revered to this day for his great contribution to people who sought complete liberation. He was not an idol, but more a well-respected hero who had the passion to impart his own experiences to inspire others. He is exalted for his real-life contributions, not praised like other idols would be in the case of a religion.

John Baskin

Buddhism as a way of life is the training of the mind to identify the roots of suffering and eliminating them for the purpose of attaining the ultimate goal of true happiness. To take the path towards the end goal means eliminating suffering by focusing on positively changing one's self. Becoming a Buddhist is a decision to deliberately avoid suffering by dissolving notions of craving and personal wants. In summary, the belief lies in the theory that every being is subject to natural laws. The Buddhist theory suggests that the existence of inanimate and animate beings is in a state of flux. It further theorizes the infinite cycle of birth and death.

In a nutshell, Buddhism relates all of these concepts to promote moral responsibility, tolerance, wisdom, and compassion. All these qualities are believed by Buddhists to be the way to inculcate a truly meaningful life in today's world.

Teaching 2:   Understanding the Mind

"The mind is everything. What you think you become." -
Siddhartha Gautama

The Buddhist philosophy on the mind provides for a very unique definition that categorizes it as a non-physical phenomenon. Simply put, the Buddhists believe that the "brain" is the physical, while the "mind" is beyond the physical brain.

The mind perceives, thinks, and correspondingly reacts to that which happens to the environment. Buddha thought that all things are preceded by the mind, led by the mind, and created by the mind. Everything originates from the mind and every other chain of events in the environment is an offspring that derives from how the mind works.

Further Buddhist studies pertained to "clarity and knowing" as the two main aspects of the mind. The mind is clear for it has no physical form but has the ability to reflect on anything. This just means that the mind allows for anything to arise within it while it consciously engaging with objects to know and be aware of them.

With the mind and the body working together, an individual can positively react to the environment. The body, with the use of its senses, serves as the mind's vehicle towards knowing what happens in the outside world. The mind is capable of assessing what should be done and how the physical body must react.

As it is beyond physical, the mind does not expire unlike the body. It needs nourishing and development in order to stay clear and aware. This is mainly the doctrine that explains why study and meditation is important. In his teachings, Buddha provided for the ways to improve the mind.

Buddha incorporated the virtuous mental factors that must always be honed. These would include conscientiousness, faith, and a sense of propriety, consideration, non-violence and equanimity. These virtues guide the mind to clearly think and positively dictate everything originating from it.

Every teaching of Buddhism originates from the concept of the mind, regarding it as the center of everything that happens thereafter in the life of the individual.

Teaching 3: The Nature of Reality

"Do not accept any of my words on faith, believing them just because I said them. Be like an analyst buying gold, who cuts, burns, and critically examines his product for authenticity. Only accept what passes the test by proving useful and beneficial in your life." - Siddhartha Gautama

Buddhism does not have an answer as to who was the creator and what the origin of the universe was, but it does believe in the concept of endless existence. For Buddhists, *Samsara, or* "endless existence" is the ultimate reality.

This theory was explained by Buddha as impermanent and ever-changing. The state of being is temporary and endless. Forms are ever in flux; yet some forms such as oceans and seas, last longer than humans. For them, the true nature of reality lies in the impermanence of everything. Elements form part of a particular animate or inanimate object, but soon after, these elements break apart and such a form will come to an end.

You will see that the rest of the teachings of Buddhism draw back from this ultimate reality. The belief is hinged on the fact that one must do his best to achieve true happiness before one ceases to exist. This is the Buddhist philosophy that explains why they do nothing that does not prove beneficial to their lives.

John Baskin

Teaching 4: The Harmonious Assembly

"It is like a lighted torch whose flame can be distributed to ever so many other torches which people may bring along; and therewith they will cook food and dispel darkness, while the original torch itself remains burning ever the same. It is even so with the bliss of the Way." - Siddhartha Gautama

Like a lighted torch, an enlightened individual is supposed to spread his fire to others. This is part of the path towards true enlightenment. Buddha envisioned an awakened community that embodies the teachings of Buddhism. To continue to live by the ideals of Buddhism and spread the teachings to others, the ultimate purpose is fulfilled.

Some believers take this vow to the next level and follow Buddha's example. This explains why people who have decided to become monks have renounced their personal lives and chosen to devote themselves to the belief.

Strong believers have chosen to relinquish themselves from the worldly ways and pursued gaining wisdom that can transcend suffering. Their coming together as a community is called *Sangha* in Buddhist terms. An ordained community of monks and nuns is a harmonious assembly, coming together for the purpose of preserving the belief, while trying to propagate such belief to attract more followers.

Teaching 5: Interconnected Causations

"Nothing ever exists entirely alone; everything is in relation to everything else."

- Siddhartha Gautama

Understanding the causality in Buddhist terms means understanding the universal truth. As previously discussed, Buddhism sees that everything is interconnected to everything else. It imparts a notion of interconnectedness of every being.

Much like the teachings of other religion, Buddhism promotes co-dependence, proving to be the best reason for loving one another and respecting every being that exists together with them. This teaching simply tells us that no man is an island. It explains that we are part of a bigger picture, where everything depends on everything else.

This teaching reminds us to dispense of selfishness and embrace gratefulness for one another, for everyone is an indispensable part of one's self. It further strengthens our moral responsibility to be good to one another and to never forget our moral obligations, which will hold everything together.

Buddhists view accepting the fact that there is nothing separate from the rest as the best way to achieve joy. Unselfish acts make true peace in the world.

Teaching 6:   The Noble Truth of Dukkha

"Our life is shaped by our mind; we become what we think. Suffering follows an evil thought as the wheels of a cart follow the oxen that draws it.
Our life is shaped by our mind; we become what we think. Joy follows a pure thought like a shadow that never leaves."

- Siddhartha Gautama

The Dukkha, also known as the First Noble Truth, is suffering. For Buddhists, anything that is temporary causes suffering. To them, Dukkha must be understood in order to be surpassed.

In reality, Dukkha is a common bond that all of us share. It does not suggest pessimism, but it is a teaching that is most grounded in the reality that everybody suffers. It is factual philosophy that some believe to be neither optimistic, nor pessimistic.

Suffering varies and does not come in similar forms, yet it is something that cannot be avoided by anyone, even by those who can be considered privileged in life. On a positive note, this common bond brings a sense of compassion that makes us incapable of doing wrong to those who suffer the same suffering as we do.

Teaching 7: The Second Noble Truth: Arising of Dukkha

"What is evil? Killing is evil, lying is evil, slandering is evil, abuse is evil, gossip is evil, envy is evil, hatred is evil, to cling to false doctrine is evil; all these things are evil. And what is the root of evil? Desire is the root of evil, illusion is the root of evil."

- Siddhartha Gautama

The second noble truth relates to man's worldly desire. The "Arising of Dukkha" means to give rise to suffering. It admits that desire, greed, and thirst for impermanent pleasures will arise in our lifetime. These are regarded as the most palpable cause of Dukkha and such thirst is caused by the false idea of self-arising out of ignorance. Thirst and greed is manifested even in small personal quarrels and to big events such as wars. This suggests that all the problems in the world today boil down to our selfish superficial desires.

The reason as to why there is dukkha was not a priority for the Buddha. He was more concerned on how it can be avoided and what necessary condition would help him do so. He tried to discover simple and practical solutions to deal with dukkha. Based on his findings 2500 years ago, the bringing about of dukkha does not only include craving, but also includes being alive and conscious. He realized that craving is the only aspect of dukkha that can be dealt with because it is a by-product of the mind.

A clear and knowing mind will be able to prevent dukkha from happening because it has been enlightened by the teachings. Thus, wisdom of the mind was his best solution to prevent worldly craving and selfishness.

Teaching 8:   The Ending of Dukkha

*"May all that have life be delivered from suffering..." -
Siddhartha Gautama*

The Third Noble Truth is known as the Ending of Dukkha or the Cessation of Dukkha. It pertains to the liberation from suffering. It is more popularly known as Nibbana or Nirvana, a state of emancipation from sufferings.

This Noble Truth further discusses the way to extinguish, denounce, and detach oneself from the thirst. The goal is to extinguish the fires of greed, hatred, and delusion. Buddha suggested that suffering can be surpassed and happiness will then become attainable.

Buddha suggested to live fully by alienating obsession with selfish wants. Contentment is the best remedy to psychological suffering. To let go selfish craving, restless wanting, hatred, envy, and anger is to enjoy living life.

Helping others while staying contented in a life of simplicity is the key to fulfilling the third noble truth.

Teaching 9:   The Noble Truth of the Path to Nirvana

"When you come upon a path that brings benefit and happiness to all, follow this course as the moon journeys through the stars." - Siddhartha Gautama

The Fourth Noble Truth is also known as the 'Middle Path' or the way leading to the cessation of dukkha. It was regarded as a middle path for a simple reason that it avoids the extremes of a path that leads to happiness through the temporary pleasures of the body and happiness where happiness is achieved through self-mortification.

The Middle Path is believed to have Eightfold Path to wit:

- *Right Understanding*
- *Right Thought*
- *Right Speech*
- *Right Action*
- *Right Livelihood*
- *Right Effort*
- *Right Mindfulness*
- *Right Concentration*

Buddha was believed to have traversed the extreme path during his younger years. According to his writings, these are painful paths that lead to nothing but suffering. The Middle Path, however, suggested eight paths that must be developed simultaneously, as they complement each other.

By traversing this path to Nirvana, the essential Buddhist disciplines are being perfected by an individual. Wisdom, mental discipline, and ethical conduct compose the roadmap towards the end of the path.

Buddha emphasized the significance of complete understanding and following of the Path in order to reach Nirvana. Knowing and traversing the path is one thing, but completing is the end goal for Buddhists.

Teaching 10: Vows of Bodhisattva

"If the selflessness of phenomena is analyzed and if this analysis is cultivated, it causes the effect of attaining nirvana. Through no other cause does one come to peace." - Siddhartha Gautama

The Vows of Bodhisattva are a commitment purely for the sake of others. It is an act that is purely selfless and requires strong determination. It is a vow of pure renunciation and of an intention that involves nothing but enlightenment that benefit others.

Individual wisdom and liberation is a pre-requisite before the vow is taken. It makes perfect sense for it is only a strong mind that can endure the sacrifices of this altruistic vow. It also further believed that the vows outlive one's lifetime. This means that promise to keep the vow continues through subsequent lifetimes.

Believers suggest that in order to keep the strong commitment to fulfilling the vow, it is very important to understand that it does not put one in chains, but it is simply a decision adopted by a committed being – a mindful decision to restrain himself from negative conduct.

Teaching 11: Mahayana Path

'Whatever the highest perfection of the human heart-mind may
I realize it for the benefit of all that lives!'- Siddhartha
Gautama

The Mahayana Path is the path toward becoming a Buddha. It is pertained as the "Great Way" or the "Greater Vehicle", the path to understanding the meaning of being a Buddha and enlighten others to walking the same path.

The Path must be taken without doubts or vexations. In this path, the mind is taught absolute stillness, free from clinging and attachments. There are five pre-requisite paths to be taken to be able to take the Mahayana. These are paths of accumulation, preparation, seeing, meditation, and no more learning. Taking these five paths shall escalate the journey to the greater vehicle, the Path of Mahayana. It is said that this is the last path towards a being's journey to absolute happiness.

John Baskin

Teaching 12: The Righteous View

"If you are facing in the right direction, all you need to do is keep on walking." - Siddhartha Gautama

Although the right view is the forerunner of the Eightfold Path, it must be noted that the paths are in a particular order. The righteous view serves as the glue that sticks together all the other paths, for it marks the start of understanding. The Right View guides an individual in taking the rest of the Eightfold Path. It is the foundation of the journey to the final destination. Without a righteous view, it will be hardly possible to progress.

The Right View is similar to having a destination in mind. One can ride his vehicle and start traveling different roads, but without a place to go to, he will get lost or will not be able to go anywhere at all. In order to arrive at a desired place, Buddha thought that one should have an idea of the directions leading to it.

Further, the right view must govern our acts and our attitude when dealing with life. It is the view that will keep one's theoretical convictions intact. It gives structure to perception and values that will later on determine the way one will react to his environment.

Teaching 13: The Righteous Thought

"On the contrary, we shall live projecting thoughts of universal love to those very persons, making them as well as the whole world the object of our thoughts of universal love — thoughts that have grown great, exalted and measureless. We shall dwell radiating these thoughts which are void of hostility and ill will.' It is in this way, monks, that you should train yourselves." - Siddhartha Gautama

The Righteous Thought is also regarded in scriptures as the "right intention." The Buddha described this as the way of thinking wherein one gives up ill will and cravings. The right view is the application of the mind that yields fruitful results, leading to the enjoyment of life to the fullest.

The Buddha expounded on the definition of the Righteous Thought by providing a threefold explanation. He explained the intention of goodwill, intention of harmlessness and the intention of renunciation, in order to fully explain the meaning of a rightful intent. These three aspects correspond exactly to the negative thoughts that can enter one's mind.

The intention of renunciation does not necessarily mean that Buddhism calls for everyone to enter the monastery. It simply meant that one must resist and eventually abandon the desire; the root of all evil. Renunciation is in terms of turning back from desire to achieve freedom.

The intention of goodwill and harmlessness come together. Intention of goodwill means loving kindness that diverts anger and resentment, which stops a human being from acting on ill will. It is the intense selfless love for other beings and doing good deeds for the welfare of all. Meanwhile, the intention of harmlessness nourishes our love for others, for it is a thought guided by sincere compassion. A sense of compassion coupled with loving-kindness promotes peace and happiness within one's self.

Teaching 14: The Righteous Speech

"And what, monks, is right speech? Abstinence from false speech, abstinence from malicious speech, abstinence from harsh speech, abstinence from idle chatter: this is called right speech." - Siddhartha Gautama

The Buddha incorporated the Righteous Speech in the Eightfold Path because this is an aspect of self-discipline that can easily be disregarded by many. It is an easy offense that does not inflict direct physical damage to others, but is usually equally hurting.

The Right Speech maybe commonly ignored. This is why Buddha stressed that self-purification involves the use of well-chosen speech and avoidance of deliberate lies. One must speak only words that do no harm, those that do not bring evil to anyone.

In Buddha's teachings, he reminded the learners to reflect on their speech, before, during, and after speaking. He wanted his learners to decipher the possible effects of uttered words before even spitting them out.

The Righteous Speech does not only reflect personal virtue, but a path that may cause hate and deceit, if not fulfilled. Righteous Speech must be practiced to prevent violence and acrimony.

Teaching 15: Righteous Action

"Look not to the faults of others, nor to their omissions and commissions. But rather look to your own acts, to what you have done and undone" - *Siddhartha Gautama*

The Righteous Action discusses about the morally upright conduct that one must uphold at all times. Actions of the body must never bring harm to any human being in order to maintain harmony in life.

The Buddha listed the Ten Commandments to ensure righteous action, to wit:

"1.   Refrain from taking the life of any being

2.   Refrain from taking what is not freely given

3.   Refrain from inappropriate sexual conduct

4.   Refrain from lying

5.   Refrain from divisive speech

6.   Refrain from using harsh words

7.   Refrain from idle talk (gossip)

8.   Refrain from coveting other's possessions and positions

9.   Refrain from resenting the good fortune of others

10.   *Refrain from holding a closed mind about things one doesn't fully understand"*

These were the precepts that Buddha suggested to ensure only rightful actions of the body. Right actions are influenced by right intentions and right views. This is why the path to Righteous Action always coincides with the other Eightfold Path.

Teaching 16: The Righteous Way of Making a Living

"To practice Right Livelihood, you have to find a way to earn your living without transgressing your ideals of love and compassion. The way you support yourself can be an expression of your deepest self, or it can be a source of suffering for you and others. "- Siddhartha Gautama

Buddha sees making a living as an expression of one's deepest self. He anticipated that man would still need a livelihood to live. As it is admittedly a need that cannot be relinquished from one's life, Buddha suggested that followers must find a way to earn a living without compromising ideals of love and compassion.

What the Buddha tried to explain is that making a living is a compulsory requirement to survival in this world, but more than this, he is encouraging men to engage in a livelihood that is ethically positive, does not do harm to others, and can ideally complement the journey you take towards enlightenment.

Teaching 17: Righteous Effort and Vitality

"I shall not give up my efforts until I have attained whatever is attainable by manly perseverance, energy, and endeavor." - *Siddhartha Gautama*

The Righteous Effort is a mental discipline suggested to keep doing what is right and continue renouncing the wrong. Effort, vitality, and energy comes one path, for they all comprise the righteous effort, as pertained by Buddha in the scriptures.

Energy is a significant factor towards fulfilling the right effort. It fuels one's mind to exert effort and act in guidance of the right intentions. Energy liberates the mind to produce the needed effort for diligence and perseverance.

In Buddhist belief, an individual works for his own deliverance. For this task, energy is a significant requirement for the cultivation of the mind. Effort is needed until the end goal is attained. Buddha provided for the following kinds of effort needed to enlightenment:

1. Effort to prevent unwholesome qualities.
2. Effort to extinguish existing unwholesome qualities.
3. Effort to cultivate wholesome qualities that have not yet arisen.
4. Effort to enhance wholesome qualities that are already present.

These four kinds of effort are required to progress and be one step closer the end goal.

Teaching 18: Righteous Awareness

"Wakefulness is the way to life.
The fool sleeps
As if he were already dead,
But the Master is awake
And he lives forever.

He watches.
He is clear.

How happy he is!
For he sees that wakefulness is life.
How happy he is,
Following the path of the awakened.

With Great perseverance
He meditates, seeking
Freedom and happiness. "
- Siddhartha

The path to complete awareness is a path of mindfulness of everything that happens within one's self and those that happen to be in the world around him. It speaks about an overall consciousness of himself and of the world outside.

More than that, right awareness requires focus at all times. Mindfulness of everything does not mean getting involved or becoming attached to all things around. It simply implies that with right awareness, one can easily learn to deal with anything with more peace of mind. It should develop more wisdom through having insights into the nature of things and events happening around the individual. This way, inner stability is achieved.

Teaching 19: Righteous Level of Consciousness

"Awake. Be the witness of your thoughts.

You are what observes, not what you observe" - Siddhartha Gautama

Right level of consciousness or Right Concentration implies that one can dictate what is worthy and useful for his concentration. It is a path where concentration affords us to see things as they really are, and not what they are purported to be.

With this level of concentration, we attain a joyful peace of mind that helps us appreciate all beings around us. It inculcates our love for ourselves and for one another.

These concepts are the reasons for many original rituals created today. The goal is to achieve a level of concentration that purifies the mind.

Teaching 20: Reincarnation

"Every morning we are born again. What we do today is what matters most." - Siddhartha Gautama

In the teaching of Buddhism, it must be noted that there is no "soul or self." Contrary to the common notion of reincarnation, where the body transforms into another form or another body after death, Buddhism teaches a different view that focuses on impermanence of beings.

Buddhists believe that there is no beginning to birth, but there is an end to it. The end of rebirth happens when destructive emotions prevail. Meanwhile, the concept of the mind-stream remains. The Buddhist theory on reincarnation also provides for the past and the future lives or past and future rebirths.

Rebirth happens in two ways: one, under the command of destructive emotions, and the other comes with the power of compassion. Prayers also play an important role in rebirth.

Teaching 21: Karma

"What you are is what you have been. What you'll be is what you do now." - Siddhartha Gautama

Karma is one of the forerunning doctrines of Buddhism that is popular even to mere spectators. The concept of Karma or moral causation which means that anything one does today, either good or bad, will have consequences in the future series of events in his lifetime. Karma does not only pertain to past actions. It encompasses both the past and the present act. The Buddha has always emphasized that we create our own happiness or misery, and this concept of Karma is the best explanation to that claim.

What is not popularly understood is that Karma is not the only mechanism that determines the future. It is only one of the mechanisms that affect what may happen in the future. It is also not "fate" imposed by an Almighty being, which is not considered to be part of Buddhist belief. It is a mere consequence of an action like how Sir Isaac Newton's Third Law of Motion was explained. Every action brings about equal and opposite reaction.

Teaching 22: Renunciation

"A man asked Gautama Buddha, "I want happiness."
Buddha said, "First remove "I," that's Ego, then remove "want,"
that's Desire.
See now you are left with only "Happiness." - Siddhartha
Gautama

In layman's terms, "Renunciation" means "to leave" or "relinquish." However, it suggests a deeper meaning from the Buddhist perspective. For them, Renunciation is tantamount to Liberation from the lusts of the world. It is the liberation from wanting and desire. More so, Renunciation may mean the extreme of entirely leaving the worldly ways and entering the monastery like the Buddhist monks do.

In a more general Buddhist perspective, Renunciation is understood as the "act of letting go of ignorance and suffering." Buddha suggested that it is the way to avoid attachment and wanting, where the road to enlightenment shall become clearer.

In his writings, the Buddha understood that not everyone can devote their lives to living in a monastery and admitted that physical possessions will be realized with hard work. For laymen, it is enough to not cling to or be obsessed with the pleasures of the physical world.

Teaching 23: Compassion

"... But, ancient wisdom has advocated a different timeless strategy to overcome hatred. This eternal wisdom is to meet hatred with non-hatred. The method of trying to conquer hatred through hatred never succeeds in overcoming hatred. But, the method of overcoming hatred through non-hatred is eternally effective. That is why that method is described as eternal wisdom. " - Siddhartha Gautama

The Buddhist view on compassion demands a higher level of sympathy with others. It is more than the emotions attached to sympathizing with other beings. For a Buddhist, compassion means the willingness to bear the pain of others. This belief draws back from another familiar teaching that tells us about our interdependence on one another.

Further, the idea of true compassion does not expect anything in exchange. True compassion comes without any reward, including being thanked for whatever we have done. It is plainly sacrificing for others.

For many Buddhists, compassion also means the solidarity of the heart. It is the desire to relieve oneself from suffering and give joy to other beings. Genuine compassion entails helping others to overcome their sufferings, because their happiness forms part of your own.

Teaching 24: Bodhichitta

"Hatred never ceases by hatred
But by love alone is healed.
This is an ancient and eternal law." - Siddhartha Gautama

Bodhichitta literally means, "mind of enlightenment", an altruistic mind that beings must aspire to have. In Buddhism, it is the finest of all spiritual objectives. A mind of enlightenment puts oneself last and puts forward the welfare of other beings first.

The Ultimate Bodhichitta is linked to having wisdom and compassion held together. Although, in some scriptures, it is solely equated with compassion, Buddha believed that wisdom nourishes compassion and vice versa.

Genuine emotions prove possession of a genuine heart that can feel true genuine compassion. For Buddhists, a genuine heart and an enlightened mind must be shared with all. The Buddha encourages us all to train ourselves to fully embrace Bodhichitta even if unpredictable encounters, triggering fear and anger, come into our daily paths.

John Baskin

Teaching 25: Emptiness

"How blissful it is, for one who has nothing. Attainers-of-wisdom are people with nothing. See him suffering, one who has something, a person bound in mind with people." - Siddhartha Gautama

Emptiness is not similar to the popular notion of nothingness and hollowness. In Buddhism, it explains a way of looking at experiences. It is a way of thinking, suggesting that we are to look at events with utmost purity and without any underlying motives behind them.

The concept of emptiness also further strengthens the Buddhist view of impermanence and constant evolution. In Buddhist traditions, one who is in harmony with emptiness is in harmony with all things. When emptiness is embraced by an individual, peace comes thereafter. He no longer separates himself or other beings from one another. With full acceptance of emptiness, he liberates not only himself, but all other beings as well.

In layman's terms, emptiness pertains to being selfless. An individual with full grasp of this concept removes the concept of "I" in order to attain peace in life.

Teaching 26: Keeping the Links to the Truth: The Bodhisattva Vows

"I teach suffering, its origin, cessation and path. That's all I teach"- Siddhartha Gautama

In the previous discussion of the Bodhisattva Vows, it was explained that it is a path attained by a person with great compassion or one who has adopted the purpose of attaining enlightenment for the benefit of all other beings. The path is said to be one's link to the Ultimate Truth. Keeping the vow is not an easy task even for those who have promised themselves to fulfill it. Thus, knowing how to keep the vow is as important as embracing it.

Buddhists understand that the need to practice the six perfections of discipline, patience, giving, concentration, effort, and wisdom is the only way to keep the vows. The vows serve as an everyday weapon for us to cut through all kinds of suffering around us.

It is also believed that keeping the vows benefits us, like a wish-granting charm, a precious jewel that shall help us obtain happiness for others and ourselves.

John Baskin

Teaching 27: Respect of Living Beings

*"The forest is a peculiar organism of unlimited kindness
and benevolence that makes no demands for its
sustenance and extends generously the products of its
life activity; it affords protection to all beings, offering
shade even to the axe-man who destroys it." -
Siddhartha Gautama*

Part of the Five Precepts of Buddhism is the respect for living beings. The Precepts provides for the guidelines on the Buddhist way of living that is moral and guided by wisdom. They serve as the preliminary requisites or the groundwork that must be done on a daily basis.

The first precept is self-explanatory. Buddhists believe that all living beings deserve love and respect, human or not. Killing any living being, either by one's own hands, or by influencing another, is disrespect to another's life.

Buddhists strongly believe that even non-humans have equal right to live. Incorporating this to the concept of Karma, killing other life forms shall deliver us ill health and misfortune. Loving kindness and protection of life must be cultivated in order to achieve true happiness.

Teaching 28: To Not Take What is Not Given

"The non-doing of any evil,

the performance of what's skillful,

the cleansing of one's own mind:

this is the teaching of the Awakened. " - Siddhartha Gautama

Second to the Five Precepts is also something that even other beliefs practice. It is the respect to one's right to own property. Like the general rules on morality, Buddhists believe that if something is not given, it should not be taken. To take such property from another is either stealing or fraud. Any form of stealing or fraud is condemned by Buddhism, including even the smallest act of non-observance of generosity, which counts as fraud.

Now, going back, the main objective of this Precept is to harness the virtue of generosity amongst all. Material and non-material gifts to another, including an offering of sympathy, is a gift that one person can offer to another. Happiness is said to be invited by those who generously give to others.

Teaching 29: Sexual Misconduct

"Through the round of many births I roamed without reward,
without rest, seeking the house-builder.

Painful is birth again & again.

House-builder, you're seen!
You will not build a house again.
All your rafters broken,
the ridge pole destroyed,
gone to the Unformed,
the mind has come to the end of craving." - Siddhartha
Gautama

Avoiding sexual misconduct is believed to keep us away from having undesirable partners and enemies, for it is an indication that one does not have respect for his personal relationships with other beings.

Unlike the common misconceptions, it is not written in Buddhist scriptures that one has to practice celibacy in order to attain happiness. It does direct us to loyalty and faithfulness to relationships and to not engaging in any mentally or physically hurtful sexual conduct that proves disrespect toward others.

Teaching 30: False Speech

"The tongue like a sharp knife... Kills without drawing blood." -
Siddhartha Gautama

Respect for the truth is of high importance to Buddhist views. Buddha believed that nothing positive can be expected from telling lies. Half-truths are also not acceptable because, in the same way, it undermines the virtue of truthfulness.

Truthfulness and honesty are the main ingredients of understanding. Half-truths are regarded as no different from telling lies. This precept provides us with a very clear, yet hard task to fulfill on a daily basis.

Teaching 31: Confusion of the Mind

"There is nothing more dreadful than the habit of doubt. Doubt separates people. It is a poison that disintegrates friendships and breaks up pleasant relations. It is a thorn that irritates and hurts; it is a sword that kills." - Siddhartha Gautama

In laymen's term, Confusion of the Mind is the act or habit of taking intoxicants to alter emotions and way of thinking. This practice goes directly against the Buddhist perspective on wisdom.

Apart from infringing on one's health, taking of intoxicants makes us vulnerable to embrace evil. Thus, even if drinking alcohol or taking drugs does not necessarily hurt or violate others, our own mental health is jeopardized. We lose control and we are exposed to the high possibility of breaking the other tenets of the right way of living.

Clarity of the mind is a requirement to achieve wisdom. Avoiding anything that confuses the mind, thus, contributes to our overall peace of mind and in keeping the vows of living an enlightened life.

Teaching 32: The Ten Paramita

"Long is the night to him who is awake; long is a mile to him who is tired; long is life to the foolish who do not know the true law." - Siddhartha Gautama

The Ten Paramita, widely known as the "Ten Perfections" are qualities Buddha believed to be possessed by each one of us. These are the qualities that one must continuously live to possess in order to attain Buddhahood.

The following qualities are what that we need to practice in our everyday lives:

- *Generosity*
- *Virtue*
- *Renunciation*
- *Discernment*
- *Equanimity*
- *Patience*
- *Persistence*
- *Truth*
- *Determination*
- *Goodwill*

One must have the will to achieve these qualities in order to achieve them. Our own awakening depends solely on ourselves. Buddha taught that these qualities must be harnessed, while we abandon unskillful ones. It is our own decision to take the right path in life that shall bring upon the realization of our own awakening. No one else can do it for us.

Teaching 34: Metta

"Those who attempt to conquer hatred by hatred are like warriors who take weapons to overcome others who bear arms. This does not end hatred, but gives it room to grow. But, ancient wisdom has advocated a different timeless strategy to overcome hatred. This eternal wisdom is to meet hatred with non-hatred. The method of trying to conquer hatred through hatred never succeeds in overcoming hatred. But, the method of overcoming hatred through non-hatred is eternally effective. That is why that method is described as eternal wisdom. " - Siddhartha Gautama

The first of the four sublime states of the mind is "Metta". Before we discuss Metta, we must first understand that the four sublime states are the qualities of the mind that alleviate suffering. It is also referred to as the *uplifted state of the mind* that embodies Buddhism's core teachings.

Metta, in Buddhist scriptures, is referred to as "boundless friendliness." In a more popular sense, it is known as "loving kindness." It is explained as the act of wishing well for others as much as we wish well for ourselves.

We can refer back to the discussion of the concept of compassion in order to fully understand Metta, which ultimately enriches our love for ourselves and all other sentient beings. In Buddhism, the highest form of love is Metta, the kind of love that is strength and gives strength.

Teaching 35: Karuna

"Imagine that every person in the world is enlightened but you. They are all your teachers, each doing just the right things to help you learn perfect patience, perfect wisdom, perfect compassion." - Siddhartha Gautama

Everyone have their own sufferings and most of the times, our own pain deafens us. Our selfishness makes unaware of others. This is why Karuna, or compassion, is the Buddhists' way to liberate a narrow heart, to one that is wide as the world.

For Buddha, the true sense of Karuna takes away the heaviness of the heart. It is a quality that can reconcile us to our own destiny by making us aware that the lives of other are far harder than ours.

It is true that sorrow has the same taste for all of us and it is one that we all share. This is why we must strengthen Karuna in order to help others, and ourselves get through our hardships by helping each other.

Teaching 36: Mudita

"Let us rise up and be thankful, for if we didn't learn a lot at least we learned a little, and if we didn't learn a little, at least we didn't get sick, and if we got sick, at least we didn't die; so, let us all be thankful." - Siddhartha Gautama

Mudita is the so-called antidote to envy. It is best translated as "the joy one feels in the joy of others". Buddha believed that we could gain more joy by sharing the happiness of others, as if it is our own.

In Buddhism, sympathetic joy is the highest form of joy that one can achieve. This is the best proof that we have successfully removed the concept of "I" in our minds and a proof that we believe that our interdependence with other beings is undeniable.

Teaching 37: Upekkha

"Praise and blame, gain and loss, pleasure and sorrow come and go like the wind. To be happy, rest like a giant tree in the midst of them all" - Siddhartha Gautama

Upekkha means equanimity. It is the last sublime state that discusses a perfectly balanced, steady, and calm mind. By far, it is the most realistic of the Four Sublime States for it prepares us for reality.

It is the teaching that tells us that balance of mind is the best armor to face the ups and downs of life. It is realistically sound because it compels us to prepare ourselves to accept the fact that life is not easy. Upekkha provides us an antidote to stress because this quality anticipates both the pleasant and the unpleasant surprises of life.

The idea of Upekkha in Buddhism helps us face the truths in life and helps us respond to life's continuous contrast of rise and fall. As we train ourselves to attain Upekkha, we become stronger against the vicissitudes of life.

Teaching 38: The Five Spiritual Faculties

"Wakefulness is the way to life.
The fool sleeps
As if he were already dead,
But the Master is awake
And he lives forever.

He watches.
He is clear.

How happy he is!
For he sees that wakefulness is life.
How happy he is,
Following the path of the awakened.

With Great perseverance
He meditates, seeking
Freedom and happiness. " - Siddhartha Gautama

In terms of spiritual progress, the Buddha believed in the five cardinal rules to follow to ensure that we do not merely respond on sense-based instincts and impulses. The five cardinal rules must take over and govern how we feel, think, and act in our everyday life.

Faith, vigor, mindfulness, concentration, and wisdom are the five core virtues that one must have. Faith keeps us in touch with our perspectives and beliefs in life. Vigor gives us the vitality to project ourselves positively in any given situation. Mindfulness makes us aware of the truths of life. Concentration helps us focus on keeping the good and dispensing the bad. Wisdom is the key to liberating ourselves and achieving happiness that extends to all beings.

These five faculties go together as one. This means we must develop each and not leave any one of them unaccomplished. For Buddhists, the higher the degree of development of each faculty means the higher degree of enlightenment.

John Baskin

Teaching 39: Challenges to the Awakening

"There is nothing more dreadful than the habit of doubt. Doubt separates people. It is a poison that disintegrates friendships and breaks up pleasant relations. It is a thorn that irritates and hurts; it is a sword that kills." - Siddhartha Gautama

Buddhahood is a lifetime commitment to the vows of enlightenment. It is the consistent training of wisdom and practice of ethics, coupled with sustained meditation. It is one of the most challenging and rewarding experience that one can ever have. The process may be slow, but it should be steady. With a lot of patience and determination, it is truly achievable for anyone.

Although the struggles to face in our lives have become much harder in modern times, it is still not an impossible thing to overcome. Some would say that it is both a blessing and a curse to be awakened. It is a blessing because it rewards us with true happiness, yet it is a curse, in a way that one must be willing to walk away from most of the things that the physical world offers. The challenges that come along the path to awakening are seriously hard to avoid, especially if we have already been exposed to the pleasures of the material world.

Buddhists believe that the best way to overcome the challenges, apart from having a strong will to take the path, is to surround ourselves with others who are taking the same road to enlightenment. The challenges become easier to bear.

Meanwhile, on a positive note on the challenges in the road to awakening, we can say that without the challenges, the path to

56

enlightenment will never feel complete. The triumph over evil ways brings upon added joy to one's heart.

Teaching 40: Mindfulness of the Body

"Your purpose in life is to find your purpose and give your whole heart and soul to it" - Siddhartha Gautama

Mindfulness of the Body is a way to detach ourselves from suffering. It is a state of keen curiosity that makes us pay attention to what is happening within our own temples. It is a very good way of maintaining bodily health and emotional strength.

Once we become mindful of our body, we become fully aware of our actions and our way of reacting to external factors surrounding us. Thus, it is a tool of focus that delivers us from doing what is not upright and virtuous.

Mindfulness of the body pertains taking control of our responses in any given situation. It is a form of control, proving that we are in touch of our immediate physical experiences.

Teaching 41: Mindfulness of Sensations

"Though one should live a hundred years without wisdom and control, yet better, indeed, is a single day's life of one who is wise and meditative." - Siddhartha Gautama

Mindfulness of bodily sensations means that we have a high level of awareness of whatever we presently feel in our body. These sensations are association with not just what is physically going on within our bodies, but they are influenced by emotions, memories, states of mind, and other thoughts that concern us. Now, to say that we are mindful of our bodily sensations means that we are able to suppress our negative aversions.

Mindfulness of sensations provides us the benefit of being more aware of ourselves. The idea is that as we become mindful of these sensations, we gain insight. By gaining insight, we realize that everything is impermanent. With this realization, we will be able to let pass and let go our negative reactions and we can finally detach ourselves from suffering.

John Baskin

Teaching 42: Mindfulness of Consciousness

"A man is not called wise because he talks and talks again; but if he is peaceful, loving and fearless then he is in truth called wise." - Siddhartha Gautama

Consciousness, as previously discussed, is an effort to keep track of our mind-states. The Buddhist way to maintaining mindful consciousness is to look beyond the surface of our experiences. One needs to extend effort to understand how his own mind functions.

In Buddhist traditions, spending time with oneself is one way of strengthening consciousness. Engaging in mental training makes it possible for us to change the way our minds work. Now, going back to the concept of the oneness of the body and mind, it is said that consciousness changes the mind, while the mind changes the body. This is mainly why this aspect of mindfulness is regarded as a sign of a healthy mind.

Teaching 43: Mindfulness of All Phenomena

"Words do not express thoughts very well; everything immediately becomes a little different, a little distorted, a little foolish. And yet it also pleases me and seems right that what is of value and wisdom of one man seems nonsense to another." -
Siddhartha Gautama

Mindfulness of All Phenomena is the totality of all the antidotes to the vicious cycle of suffering. It is a state where one is able to achieve a sense of clarity in the way we see ourselves and other sentient beings.

With the application of the four mindful practices, we become aware, even of our misunderstandings. Mindfulness of all phenomena disproves all the habitual misunderstanding that bring us doubts and fear. With this, we train ourselves to claim the unlimited benefit of joy and peace.

John Baskin

Teaching 44: Brief History of Buddhism

"If we could see the miracle of a single flower clearly our whole life would change." - Siddhartha Gautama

It is believed that the origins of Buddhism go back to the 5th century B.C.E., somewhere in Northern India. Siddhartha Gautama lived to show that world that enlightenment could be achieved. During the 1st century B.C.E., his journey was put into writing in order to spread the word of wisdom to all.

A very popular story on the origins of Buddhism and the start of the Buddha's journey is his experience of near-starvation when he discovered the art of meditation. From thereon, Buddha spent long years in pursuing his newly discovered path. He had made himself an example for others. From there on, he had made his own experiences a basis for truth.

Teaching 45: Development of Buddhism

"You are the community now. Be a lamp for yourselves. Be your own refuge. Seek for no other. All things must pass. Strive on diligently. Don't give up." - Siddhartha Gautama

During Buddha's lifetime, he established a community that soon after continued his pursuits. With a very humble beginning, Buddhism became a fully-fledged religion when the Mauryan Emperor Ashoka made it the state religion of India. He encouraged missionary activities and contributed as well to the spread of Buddhist beliefs.

As the belief spread, different interpretations to Buddha's teachings arose. The absence of a definitive structure of the religion paved way to fragmentation. Other Buddhist Schools were formed shortly after, which believed in the core teachings, but varied in the intricate applications of such teachings.

The spread of Buddhism in Asia started when trade routes were opened. The teachings would also cross oceans as the Buddhist monks traveled to pursue their paths, with the driven motive to spread the teaching to others. From that time onward, millions of people were moved and encouraged to seek the path of ultimate happiness.

Teaching 46: The Modern Day Buddha

"The one who has conquered himself is a far greater hero than he who has defeated a thousand times a thousand men." -
Siddhartha Gautama

The Modern Day Buddha is one who continues to live by the core values of Buddhism, despite the many temptations of the modern world. He acknowledges that the modern world continues to change. He is aware of these changes and he screens the good from evil.

A modern-day Buddha believes in all of the teachings and maintains the balance of life by embracing the Buddhist ways whenever he is required to respond to the events happening around him.

Although the modern Buddha normally maintains life outside the monastery, he does not allow himself to succumb to the temptations of the world. He may not have taken himself away from the world, but he has certainly mastered the balance between necessities and mere desires. The Modern Day Buddha embodies the teachings and still tries to impart these teachings to others who have not experienced the kind of happiness he gained from a virtuous life.

Teaching 47: Meditation and Practice

"A generous heart, kind speech, and a life of service and compassion are the things which renew humanity." -
Siddhartha Gautama

Meditation is a way to develop the mind. It serves as exercise and the way of shaping our own minds. It is an essential way to keep the vigor of our mental wellbeing. Meditation techniques help us to further our ability to focus, keep our minds calm, and to act positively at all times. It provides us with a way of knowing who we are.

Meditation must be done gradually, and at a pace wherein the mind will be able to truly focus, and not get even more confused. There are a lot of ways to learn to meditate. It is not necessary to enroll in meditation classes, since keeping focus can never be taught. It is a decision that must be taken within you in order achieve.

Today, meditation is suggested to those who experience stress on a daily basis. Meditation is now popularly known as an exercise for good health and mental well being. Not many of us are aware that this practice traces its roots from the Buddha's own experience in life.

Teaching 48: Buddhism and Yoga

"When we don't have what we want, we are unhappy; when we do get what we don't want, we are unhappy. Freedom comes when we are free from our wants, our preferences." -
Siddhartha Gautama

Yoga, as we know it today, is commonly associated with Buddhism. A mind that is focused is a better tool for enlightenment. For this reason, it is better to include Yoga in discussing the ways to achieve a more focused mind that Buddhism suggests to be one key to achieving true happiness.

More than that, Yoga is closely associated to Buddhism because the Buddha was once a practitioner of yoga, as part of his pursuits to understanding of philosophy. Yoga means to cease to identify the fluctuations of the mind. Yogic schools of thought affirm most of Buddhist beliefs, especially in terms of liberation of the mind.

By practicing the Buddhist ways and using Yoga as an exercise of the mind and body, one gets closer to harnessing a free mind. With this, everything follows, including that eternal bliss that we all hope to reach.

Teaching 49: Post-Enlightenment Life

"If a traveler does not meet with one who is his better, or his equal, let him firmly keep to his solitary journey; there is no companionship with a fool." - Siddhartha Gautama

After six long years of meditation, the Buddha finally reached enlightenment. He was said to have remained in the same place where he found enlightenment while he thought about what he was bound to do next.

Of course, the Buddha initially found it difficult to deal with a world that was full of desires. Then, he began to realize that an enlightened individual must continue spreading the truth. For him, it was imperative to teach others and rescue them from suffering.

With this example, Buddhists believe that life after enlightenment must be a life of service to others. Post-enlightenment life is a life of sharing and spreading loving kindness and compassion to others. Some Buddhists also believe that the best way to keep the enlightenment is to leave the world and devote themselves in monasteries, where they can pursue Nirvana as a community.

John Baskin

Teaching 50: You, Buddhism, and the World Today

"Following the Noble Path is like entering a dark room with a light in the hand; the darkness will all be cleared away, and the room will be filled with light." - Siddhartha Gautama

Understanding all the 50 teachings tackled in this book is easy, yet the application of these teachings into our lives is something that needs motivation. Buddhism maybe seen as an extreme practice for some of us, but with deeper understanding, we will realize that the teachings are simple and realistic.

In our modern society, practicing some of the precepts are truly challenging, especially considering that we live in a world that is very much consumed by superficial pleasures. We must remember that, like us, Buddha lived in a time when a lot was happening in the world around him. With determination and realizations based on experiences, he was able to find a way to free himself from doubts, fears, and sufferings. This must also be our goal for ourselves.

To follow his lead will never bring harm. Most of the core teachings of Buddhism conform to social and moral ethics of our time. None of the Buddhist beliefs leads us astray, or suggest that we disbelieve existing laws and norms. Buddha's vision of peace and harmony is what we mostly need in these times.

The challenge is to take it upon ourselves to adopt those that are viable keys to our own happiness. The challenge of Buddhism is not about devoting ourselves like monks did, but to practice to

68

live by a life of selflessness. Most of us see ourselves alone, thus making it hard to live let alone suffer for others.

Buddhism as way of life is a logical pathway to a life of steadfast joy. As we conform to just ways, we develop a better sense of understanding of others and ourselves. True happiness is of our own making and no one else can do it for us. In the end, we only need to reflect on ourselves in order to know what it is that can make us truly happy. Definitely, Buddhism will prove us right that superficial and temporary pleasures will not count in the determination of our ultimate joy.

John Baskin

Part 2: Understanding Buddhism

The succeeding chapters in Part 2 of this book present you with an overview of Buddhism. Though there could be no book in the world that can fit all the information of all the schools, traditions and sub sects of Buddhism, the next chapters will provide you with a condensed version of the larger categories from which the smaller schools belong to.

Also there are varying texts, scriptures and translations that have been made over time, not to mention the oral transmissions that have not even been put into writing. There are also conflicts texts within Buddhist scriptures. A piece of information in the succeeding chapters may also be inconsistent in another source of information. However, as you will later know, Buddhism is not overly concerned with which school you will choose, or which tradition you will follow, instead the focus in your personalized path toward Enlightenment. The schools or traditions are guides not commandments.

It is important to learn the very origins, the founder, doctrines and teachings of Buddhism, regardless of the school or tradition that you choose. A solid foundation is needed for your future practice of Buddhism.

John Baskin

Chapter 1: History of Buddhism

Origins

Buddhism and its philosophies predate most of the major world religions today, with origins that can be traced back more than 600 hundred years B.C. Although the religion has been developed into different movements and traditions, the differences only reflects the expansion it has achieved in its millennia of existence.

No discussion of the origins of Buddhism can be complete without mention of its founder, Siddhartha Gautama. Born in ancient India, now present day Nepal, Siddhartha was a prince of high caste. To say that the circumstances of his life are subject of debate will be an understatement. No scholar has ever claimed to know the exact specifics of his life. Both the date of his birth all the way to his death is still uncertain. One of the most popular stories that tell of his life was that it was filled with omens, miracles and other mysteries. Some accounts even suggest that he was born without pain and did not require food, medicine or sleep.

His name Siddhartha means "he who achieves his aim" and that he truly did. During the celebrations for his birth, seers predicted that he will either be a great king or a great holy man. His father, wanting him to follow his footsteps and became a great king, was said to have surrounded the young prince with the life fit for a prince. Constructing more than three palaces for him, the young prince knew only joy and happiness. He was also restricted from receiving any religious teaching.

When he left one of the palaces, the young prince came across an old man. This was the first time that he was faced with aging. From then on, he left the palace more often and his father could no longer hide the sick, the old and suffering from the prince. He left his life as a prince and began his life of meditation. After a long period of fasting, records suggest 49 days and while sitting under a Bodhi tree, he was said to have attained Enlightenment. The prince, turned mendicant, turned yogi has now become Buddha. From then he spent the rest of his life teaching the insights he learned during his meditations.

Deities & Cosmology

Devas are the closest concept of deities in Buddhism. In contrast to most religions, these deities are also subject to karma, to life, death and rebirth albeit in a higher states of existence. They do not have great importance on the life of a human because they are unnecessary in the path of Enlightenment. However, these deities act to protect humans, who live a very religious lifestyle.

Deities are said to be able to transfer their good karma to humans who give offerings and worship them.

In fact most scholars suggest that divinity and Buddhism are two incompatible concept. In Buddhism, each person is charged with his own path towards Enlightenment and can achieve it independent of any deity. Buddha is simply a teacher to humans, he did not create the world or the realms, and he does not save people from the suffering of the world and does not issue judgment. The study of origins, creations and other similar concepts are considered to be shackles that can only bind someone into the ever turning wheel of fate, without being completely freed from it.

Buddhist cosmology suggests the existence of several realms and worlds. Some worlds are eternal and some are only temporary. There are worlds higher or lower compared to another represent different state of being. In each level, there are similar worlds that appear across, some numbering in the millions. These worlds do not exist independent of their own, instead they are held together by the collective karma of those who belong to it. For example, despite human and animals living in the same world, they occupy different worlds because of their differences in mental states.

There are also realms that are either formless or physical. The formless realms are occupied by beings, which also have no space or specific location. The physical realms are those with inhabitants with shape and location. For a formless being to enter a physical realm, he needs to assume a physical shape. The world, where humans live in, belongs to the earthly realms called Manusyaloka.

Religion or Philosophy

For all intents and purposes and with the teachings that you will learn in the succeeding sections of this book, Buddhism is not a religion. Most sources frequently refer to Buddhism as a religion. However calling a Buddhism a religion depends on how each person will define a religion.

For example, if you consider religion as the worship of a god, then Buddhism is definitely not a religion. Buddhism does not require prayer, worship or veneration of a god, there is simply no concept of godhood or divinity in Buddhism. The Dalai Lama is quoted for saying that Buddhism can be defined as a religion by one person and can be defined as a set of scientific beliefs for the human mind.

Most scholars regularly refer to Buddhism as a means for the concept of religion to be freed from the traditional belief of gods and other beings that possess supernatural powers. This makes Buddhism freer compared to other religions; it does not have to contend with debates about gods since it simply has no gods to begin with. Buddhism is more of a collection of exercises that teaches trains and enhances the mind than a set of rites.

Chapter 2: Branches

Within the Buddhist philosophy, there exist several branches, called schools that bear distinction from one another. Take note that there are many sub schools, sub branches, movements and other schools that reflect distinct interpretations of Buddha's teachings. For ease of discussion, there are three major schools that reflect these many sub schools.

Theravada

Roughly translated as the Teaching of the Elders, this school is mainly practiced in South and South East Asia. The teachings of this school primarily are based on the Pali Canon, the oldest of texts. While other teachings of this school have been developed over the years, they retain the Pali Canon as its foundations. This is the second largest school.

Under the teaching of the Theravadin, insight and learning are required to achieve Nirvana. In turn, these insights can only be gained through a combination of personal experience, practice of the lesson and also well thought of reasoning. Another set of teachings in this school is the concept of the Three Marks of Existence. To begin the path to Buddhahood, it is important to accept that everything is impermanent, both physical such as the body, material and properties and the immaterial such as knowledge and theories are fleeting. This is the mark of impermanence.

The second mark is that of suffering. When a person suffers, he does so because he desires things that are impermanent, such as material wealth or beauty. When the person or the objects of desire change, it causes great suffering. When a person is able to free himself from the desire of impermanent things, then he ceases to suffer. This is the mark of suffering.

The final mark is that of not-self. Each being is composed of different parts, in this school; the parts are composed of 5. The body, the sensations, the mental thoughts, the perceptions and the consciousness are the five parts. These are only parts and are not the total self. A person must be able to detach himself from these 5 parts and observe how he goes through or experiences these different parts.

Mahayana

Roughly translated as the Great Vehicle, the focus of this school is the path towards Enlightenment. It is this path which is the vehicle from which a being can transcend from his current to his highest state. In this school, the desire to achieve Enlightenment or Nirvana is considered a very superficial desire compared to a nobler aspiration, such as the desire to help all others achieve buBdhahood. This is the largest school in Buddhism today.

The concept of Boddhisattva figures greatly in this school. A boddhisattva is a being that has decided to follow the path towards Enlightenment. This decision is called bodhicitta, to achieve the nirvana as soon as possible so that the being can guide other beings to achieve it. However, in the Mahayana school, it is believed that the noblest aspiration for a boddhisattva is to delay his achievement of Nirvana until all other beings have achieved the state.

To become a boddhisattva, a person must acquire the following perfections; giving, discipline forbearance, diligence, mediation and wisdom. These perfections represent the culmination of all virtues that each represent. The more these virtues are practiced, the closer they are to perfection and the closer a being reaches Enlightenment. A being needs to practice generosity, always finding ways to give oneself to other. Proper behavior, morality and discipline must also be observed. During times of conflict, one must continue to endure and be patient. For every action done, it must be done so not grudgingly but with diligence and effort. A person must also take time to contemplate and meditate on his actions. Finally, wisdom must also be applied. These are needed to liberate not only oneself but also other beings from the suffering.

Belonging to the Mahayana school is one of the most famous sects of Buddhism, Tibetan Buddhism. The Dalai Lama of Tibet himself is associated closely with the concept of the boddhisattva. In fact, the Dalai Lama is considered to be a living Boddhisattva, who has chosen to be reincarnated in the world to guide all other beings to achieve Enlightenment. This belief clearly reflects the teachings of the Mahayana school. The achievement of Enlightenment is noble but far nobler is the desire to achieve this for the sake of helping others achieve the same.

Vajrayana

Roughly translated as the way of the thunderbolt of the diamond, this school is mainly practiced in Mongolia, Bhutan and Tibet. It is considered a branch of the Mahayana school but has gained distinction because of its specific doctrines. It focuses on the one of the three great vehicles towards achieving Enlightenment. The set of practices in this vehicle are more esoteric compared to other schools.

Figuring greatly on its teachings is the Doctrine of the Two Truth. In this belief, there are two kinds of truth, one that is relative and one that is absolute. Relative truth exists only when persons share the same truth, such as those found through common sense, consensus or similar agreements. On the other hand, absolute truth can only be perceived by the Enlightened being.

Similar to the Mahayana school, Varjayana encourages beings to achieve the state of being a Bodhisattva. To achieve this, every practitioner must seek to experience the absolute truth, through different practices. Some of these practices include meditations.

Rituals also figure greatly in this school. They are performed as the means to speed up the process or complete the path in the smallest period of time possible. One of these rituals involves esoteric transmission. In this school, premium is given to a guru and student relationship. Called a lineage, the personal or oral transmission of teachings is seen to be more valuable and effective than when learned when reading text. Only through the spoken communication of a teacher, complete with his insights and expressions, can a student fully learn the lesson.

Commonality & Differences

However, even among these thousands of sub sects there are still similarities that take the form of core philosophies. All of these schools believe that Buddha is their teacher and his teachings are the basis of their interpretations. Buddha's teachings on the Middle Way, the Four Noble Truths, the Noble Eightfold Path and the Three Marks of Existence are also accepted across all these branches. Finally Buddhahood represents the highest level of attainment and can be reached by any person whether a layperson or a monk.

There are also differences that make one school distinct from another. Some of the distinctions are found in their core teachings. For example, in the Theravada school, Arahants, beings that have reached levels of perfections, stay that way in perpetuity. The achievement of this state, beyond that of Buddhahood is the goal of every Buddhist that follows the Theravada school.

However other schools believe that even Arahants can devolve to imperfection and it is not to be the only quest of a Buddhist. Another difference is that understanding for the Theravada school does not come gradually but instead happens suddenly and all together at once. Other differences include 10 perfections for the Therevada and 6 perfections for the Mahayana. Varjayana school gives greater emphasis on rituals and practices compared to the other schools.

John Baskin

It is important to note that despite the similarities and differences of the Buddhist schools, these distinctions are not given significant importance in the practice of the philosophy. Other religions are less tolerant and more sensitive when a particular group chooses to branch out and create an interpretation of their dogma that is different from the mainstream. Among Buddhists, each being has his or her own path towards reaching Enlightenment. Choosing to take the path is all that matters in the philosophy and no criticism is given on which path is chosen.

Chapter 3: Traditions

Within the major schools of Buddhism, there are sub sects that are called Traditions. There are too many to count and more traditions are being developed as each person finds a group of people, who choose to follow and teach a similar path. The Traditions listed below are only few of the many. Again in Buddhism, there is no great significance on which tradition is right and wrong. Instead, it is important to choose a tradition that best reflects your unique journey.

Pure Land

The focus of this tradition is that on the Amitabha Buddha. Since realms are fueled by the karma of its inhabitants, the Pure Land, where the Amitabha Buddha resides, is said to be a place where the cycle of life, death and rebirth can be stopped. It is a place of beauty filled with different beings, including human beings. Due to the similarity of the Pure Land to the state of achieving Nirvana, scholars believe that the teaching of the Pure

Land tradition is very similar to the attainment of Enlightenment.

The importance of entering the Pure Land is that Amitabha Buddha and other boddhisattvas give direct instructions to the inhabitants on the final steps needed to attain Enlightenment. During the course of the instruction, the person is then given a choice whether to pursue the path or temporarily return to lower realms and help other beings reach the higher states.

One of the most well known practices in the Pure Land Tradition is that of Mindfulness. When used in congruence with Mindfulness practices, the name of the Buddha, Amitabha, is repeated over and over during the meditation. A person is then to focus on the name and devote all attention towards the name and the Buddha. Another alternative meditation is the recitation of a set of words, with a meaning that is yet to be revealed. Only when a person achieves the full effect of the meditation will the meaning of the words be revealed. The words are:

namo amitābhāya tathāgatāya tadyathā

amṛtabhave amṛtasaṃbhave

amṛtavikrānte amṛtavikrāntagāmini

gagana kīrtīchare svāhā

Zen

Zen is one of the schools that revolve most around meditative practices and application of insights for the welfare of others. There are many observations done throughout this tradition. For example, observation of the breath is done while seated.

Practitioners are directed to counting the frequency of breath and also visualizing the energy flow. Observation of the mind is also done. This time instead of the breaths, focus is given on the thoughts. The practitioner observes them and exerts little to almost no control in the flow of the thoughts.

One of the characteristics of Zen is its encouragement of group meditation. This is one of the rare times where Buddhists are enjoined to make full use of temples. Mostly it is monks who participate in this kind of meditation. Often lasting a great part of the day, practitioners remain seated for hours of meditation, broken only by meals. However, throughout the exercise, even during breaks that involve meals, work and other activities, complete mindfulness is dedicated. This practice has given rise to Zen centers, places that substitute for temples but still provide the venue needed for group meditation.

Also involved during these meditation are the chanting of sutras or songs. Often these songs are focused on a specific Boddhisattvas. In this way, the more times the names or the prayers related to the Boddhisattvas is repeated, the closer or the stronger the connection becomes with the same Boddhisattvas. These chants are usually done during special events and memorials to access the karma of these higher beings.

Shingon

One of the schools of Buddhism that focuses on the importance of lineage is the Shingon school. Buddhism elevates teachings given by one person to another higher compared to lessons learned only through the written word. This is made apparent by the Shingon, which is in itself a lineage. These are a set of teachings that are directly transmitted from one person to another.

In this tradition, it is believed that the source of the teaching, since it is orally transmitted, can be traced all the way to Buddha and his student Nagarjuna, a practitioner from India. The lineage is divided into two major branches. The lineage patriarchs are those that represent an unbroken line of transmissions and other the expounding patriarchs, those that are tasked with explain and expanding the reach of the teachings.

In fact, there are no Shingon books found in the world and all training is passed down mouth to mouth. This creates the misconception that Shingon teachings are kept secret from other people. While there is indeed some truth over the mystery of the teachings, any person can receive a lineage relationship and therefore have access to the teachings.

Rituals are also important in this school. One of the reasons why rituals are given this value is because these practices can hasten the achievement of Enlightenment. Other schools imply that reaching Enlightenment can take a soul thousands of years. However in this school, not only is the duration much shorter but also it is possible to be achieved in just one lifetime. When a combination of lineages, education between a guru and a student and a performance of the rituals are made, then Enlightenment can be achieved.

Siddham alphabet or a series of one syllable letters and symbols are at the center of the meditative practices of Shingon. A practitioner is said to have deeper insight of reality by concentrating or repeating one letter over and over again.

Tiantai

Named after the mountain where a key figure in Buddhism lived, this is a school that represents a development in Buddhism. Buddhism, originating from India, found its way farther to the East through a series of teachings carried over by gurus. When Buddhism found its way in China, it was widely accepted albeit developed to make a unique set of beliefs. Tiantai represents practices that are entirely Chinese in character.

Tiantai still shares many of its core principles with the rest of the Buddhist traditions and school, Its main difference is in its organization of the teachings. This was meant to standardize and harmonize Buddha's teaching into classifications. Central in this classification system is the Lotus Sutra. This is a verse that contains all the teachings of the Buddha, recitation of the sutra is said to bring forth a pouring of blessings. This sutra is difficult to translate because of the many versions made for it. One thing is sure however that the sutra is very long. Depending on the translation as many as 10 volumes and 28 chapters make the entire sutra.

The Tiantai classification of teachings is organized into Periods and a variety of Teachings. For example the Five Periods represent the phases in the life of Buddha and is used to guide a person throughout his own journey to Enlightenment. The Periods start with Avatamsaka, 21 days post-Enlightenment, Agamas 12 years, Vaipulya 8 years, Prajna 21 years and Nirvana 8 years. Within these periods are different teachings. From the first one is the teaching of infinite cosmology, to the truths, to a period of emptiness all the way to teachings contained in the Lotus Sutra.

The Eight Teachings also organize various doctrines and methods. These teachings include the basics, emptiness, the Bodhissattva and the Lotus Sutra. It also determines which teachings are to be given to which person, from those with medium to superior abilities to those that are taught without the student being aware of it.

Nichiren

Named after the Japanese monk who was the founder of the school, Nichiren bears the distinction of one of the few if not the only school in Buddhism that rejects other schools. This is reflected by the actions taken by Nichiren during his studies of the Buddha's teachings. According to Nichiren, his insight on the Lotus Sutra showed that other schools wrongly interpreted the path to a person has to take in Enlightenment. In public, he voiced his disagreement much to the dismay of the rulers and priests who belonged to the schools which he criticized. Nichiren was sentenced to exile and death but neither was done. Prior to his death, Nichiren chose six priests to transfer and expand his teachings. Only 5 out of 6 priests were able to transmit and create schools from Nichiren's teachings.

Similar to other schools is the importance it gives to the Lotus Sutra and its recitation. Some of its differences with other schools are the belief that every person is capable of becoming Buddha. According to this school, Buddhahood is possible for every being because every being already has an innate Buddha within them. It is only a matter of meditations, recitations and understanding and application of the doctrines can Enlightenment be achieved.

For example, Nichiren believes in the Ten Worlds. These are realms that represent circumstances a being experiences at any given moment. Knowing these realms allows one to move through them, climbing higher and higher to noblest of the realms. The basest realms are 6 and represent a being that only reacts to the world around them. The nobler realms are 4 and represent a being that actively discovers and develops insight. The realms are roughly translated as starting from Hell or total aggression, Hunger or materialism, Animality or immorality and Arrogance or selfishness. In the fifth realm, Humanity, this is where a being is becoming aware of his surroundings and is in the phase where he can cross to the higher realms. Heaven is the final lower realm where a being feels joy but only temporarily.

The nobler realms are the remaining 4. Learning is the seeking of the truth through understanding of teachings. A person must make a conscious decision to understand often from external sources such as a guru or scriptures. Next is the Realization, this is a realm or a phase where a person is starting to have an understanding of the truth albeit only partial. The next realm is the Bodhisattva, where a person realizes that his motivation must not only be attaining Enlightenment for himself but also for others. The final realm is Buddhahood, where a person is in pure joy that is permanent and independent of the world.

Tibetan

Although very similar to other schools, the Tibetan school is worth mentioning because of several reasons. First it is the only school that is considered to be a state religion of a country, Bhutan. Second is because it combines some of the most important teachings of other schools. Oral transmission is of course given value as the only way to gain a direct lineage between teacher and student. As a result, this school also takes into account the importance of devotion of the student to the teacher or guru. Another important reason to consider the Tibetan school is its encouragement of skepticism. This is very rare among other schools. Skepticism enjoins practitioners to use meditation in an analytical and critical manner. This skepticism is also applicable when choosing or listening to a guru, whether their teachings are in congruence to the teachings of Buddha.

Finally, the Tibetan school is noteworthy because of its most prominent figure. The Dalai Lama of Tibet is the most important monk in this school. As the Dalai Lama, he is supposed to have both spiritual and temporal leadership over Tibet. However, His Holiness, now living in exile in India, continues to support the autonomy of his native Tibet from the direct control of the Chinese government.

His claim to his position is in the Tibetan belief that he is the reincarnation, the fourteenth to be specific, of a Bodhisattva. Avalokitesvara, the Bodhisattva of Compassion, in his aspiration to guide all other beings to achieve Enlightenment, chose to descend to the human realm. He took form in the person of the first Dalai Lama and from then on, consciously chose the time and circumstances of his death. So great is the power of Avalokitesvara that he can determine the exact time, place and person of his next life. This is why the search for the next Dalai Lama, though deeply mysterious, can be made easy by instructions or clues left by the previous Dalai Lama.

John Baskin

Part 3: Practicing Buddhism

Buddhism is more than a set of beliefs and doctrines. In fact intrinsic and inextricable to the philosophy of Buddhism is the practice of the belief. Application is a vital part for Buddhists, only through its practice whether through solitary meditation all the way to serving and guiding others to achieve Buddhahood, are all expressions of the Buddhist belief in the form of action.

While Part 2 of this book was all about giving you information about the origins, the various schools and traditions of Buddhism, without application, all the lessons you have learned will be moot. Part 2 was meant to give you a solid foundation from which you will use as a launch pad to your application. Part 3 and the chapters succeeding are all about relating the specific principles of Buddhism and applying them into daily life.

The practice of Buddhism does not have to be in a grand or large scale. It does not have to be done in ornate temples or done in a spectacle for the senses. Most of the time, the work of Buddhists are found in the most ordinary of ways, from being mindful in your day to day life to being emphatic with your family and friends. Application can be done in the privacy of your home or in service of the need and sick. It can be done any day, any time and for and with any person.

John Baskin

Chapter 4: Samsara

Life & Death

Samsara or roughly translated as continuous movement defines the cycle of life, death and rebirth. The cycle can involve only one or all of the realms of existence. It is often a misconception that samsara is supposed to define a Buddhist, where his or her life will continue to revolve in this wheel and achieve higher and higher states of being. However, the teaching of Buddhism and in fact one of its most important tenets is not the continuation of your soul being spun in this wheel. Instead one of the objectives of the Buddhist practices is to achieve freedom from the wheel.

Beings are chained in this wheel because of several reasons. Some beings are so fixated on the material and temporary things in this world. They cling, desire or collect them and because these things are impermanent, when the things rot away, the being is left joyless and as a result tends to suffer. Instead of achieving pure joy that is independent of any external circumstances, the person is left suffering.

A being can live in any 1 of the 6 realms where the samsara spins the souls. There is the Hell realm, a place of suffering, the Hungry Ghost realm a place of extreme thirst and hunger, filled with frustration, the Animal realm, a place filled with fear, the Human realm, the current world where birth, aging, disease, death and rebirth abound. The Demi god realm is a place of constant fighting and wars and the God realm, a place filled with pleasure.

Take note that none of the 6 realms are considered to be the ideal realm; even the God realm is considered not ideal. For example, the lower 3 realms are considered too difficult to achieve Enlightenment because beings that reside there are too preoccupied with suffering. On the opposite extreme, the upper realms are too filled with pleasure that when death does arrive, beings in that realm are unprepared for it. Out of all the 6 realms, the Human realm is said to be the closest realm that can potentially provide the path of Enlightenment because both joy and suffering are present in the realm.

Improving Karma

Associated closely with the concept of samsara is karma. If samsara is a wheel then karma is the fuel that turns it. Every being accumulates his or her karma, whether good or bad. The better karma you have, the better your rebirth realm becomes, the worse your karma is, the worse your rebirth realm becomes. Similar to other principles, such as cause and effect and what you sow you shall reap, the concept of karma must be considered to achieve freedom from samsara.

Another misconception is that when you do enough good or accumulate enough good karma, you can propel yourself out of samsara and be saved from the cycle. The Buddhist principle for breaking free from samsara is to purify your karma, both good and bad. Improving karma can be done by good deeds but creating karma that can remove you from the cycle requires more than good deeds. To purify karma, you need to follow the path of Buddha.

The solution to samsara is found in the Four Noble Truth and the Noble Eightfold Path. When a person has understood and realized each of the truths, he or she is able to purify his karma and in so doing gain freedom. The Truths include: truth of suffering, its origin, it cessation and the path leading to its cessation.

The fourth Truth, the path leading to the cessation of suffering, is further divided into the eight truths. This is the realization and practice of right view, right intention, right speech, right action, right livelihood, right effort, right mindfulness and right concentration. When a being strives to perceive things as they are then it is a practice of the right view. Every motivation must come from a desire not to harm; this is a practice of right intention. Saying the truth is right speech, doing actions that are harmless is right action, engaging in good employment, business or other endeavors is right livelihood. If you continue to search for ways to improve yourself, then this is the right effort. When you exercise your consciousness and experience things as they are, then this is right mindfulness. When you perform meditation, then this is right concentration.

As you continue following these paths, you are able to improve your karma and at the same time perform good things as a result of following the paths. This is very different to the misconception that doing good deeds improves karma but instead, following the paths results to doing good deeds.

Buddhist Ethics

Outside of the clergy, Buddhism provides a basis on how to do good. These are concrete explanations or examples of how to follow the path that can be made applicable to the current times. Some practitioners are at a lost on how to apply Buddhism into specific actions steps or guidelines that can aid them in living a daily life.

Called the Five Precepts, these lay down the foundation for an ethical code of conduct for Buddhist laity. The Precepts are: abstinence from killing, from lying, from stealing, from performing sexual misconduct and finally from drinking alcohol. Although these Precepts seem to be very simple in nature, when they are applied in the modern world, a Buddhist can find almost universal applications for it. Your opinions or decisions on euthanasia, abortion, capital punishment and consumption of animal meat may be influenced by the ethical code on abstinence from killing.

While killing, lying and stealing are very definite in their interpretations, some of the precepts are still a subject of debate. For example, the abstinence of performing sexual misconduct can be interpreted in different ways. Some say that homosexuality is a perversion and therefore a kind of misconduct. Some say that since homosexuality is not specifically identified in any Buddhist text it is not considered misconduct. Some also say that misconduct constitutes sexual acts that are done out of malice, out to cause harm or out to break vows.

Another vague area is that of vegetarianism. Some say that eating meat constitutes killing. This is a subject of much debate, since there are records that Buddha himself discouraged vegetarianism and even ate meat himself. For example, the Dalai Lama upon contracting hepatitis was encouraged to eat a high protein diet. Some schools prohibit eating meat, while some allow them provided the meat they eat came from an animal that they did not personally kill. Other schools prohibit only certain kinds of meat, such as humans, elephants, dogs, tigers and other specific animals. Other schools allow eating meat but discourage that the consumption is done out of gluttony. To be a practicing Buddhist, you have to observe these set of ethics and precepts. Apply them in your daily life.

John Baskin

Chapter 5: Bodhisattva

Liberation

Another practical application of Buddhism can be found in the concept of liberation in relation to the path of a Bodhisattva. A bodhisattva is a being, who has bodhicitta, an aspiration to guide all other beings to the path of Enlightenment while wanting to achieve the same for himself. Any human has the potential to achieve this state along with actual Buddhahood. Take note that a bodhisattva is not yet a Buddha but a being already in the path of becoming a Buddhahood.

Different traditions view the path differently, some say it will take millennia for some people, while other say that it can be achieved in a lifetime. For example, Buddha referred to himself as an unenlightened bodhisatta and in the course of his life achieved Buddhahood.

There are three paths that a bodhisattva can take in his journey to Buddhahood. The King is someone who wants to achieve Buddhahood so he can use his powers to help other beings achieve the same state. The Boatman will travel with the other beings and walk hand in hand in the journey. The Shepherd will delay his own journey, while ushering others to achieve the state. Different traditions give different importance to each of the path. For example, in Theravada neither Boatman nor Shepherd is possible because you cannot guide others to attain Buddhahood when you yourself have not attained it and only the King is possible. On other hand another tradition states that the King is the basest of the path because wanting to achieve the state first before all others is seen as self-benefitting only and the Shepherd is the greatest because it represents true compassion.

Yoga

The practices of yoga are almost similar to the meditative practices of Buddhism. Although yoga originates from Hinduism, being a sister set of beliefs with Buddhism, yoga is widely practiced as an expression of Buddhist beliefs and as a path in itself towards freedom from samsara. The similarities extend all the way to the disciplines and methods used to achieve a meditative state, such as posture, breathing and concentration. The closest similarity between Hinduism and Buddhist practice is that of tantric yoga.

Here are some yoga postures that you can apply at the comforts of your home:

https://yoga.com/poses

http://www.yogajournal.com/category/poses/

http://www.health.com/health/gallery/0,,20727134_3,00.html

Meditation

Bhavana or meditation is perhaps the Buddhist practice that encompasses all schools and traditions in Buddhism. Its value is high because it is one of the tools that can unlock higher levels of awareness which are needed towards the path of Enlightenment. Buddha himself reached Buddhahood according to traditions through meditation. Both oral and written transmissions of the teachings of Buddha always have meditative instructions which are then taught to students.

Different techniques are discussed in the teachings, from achieving concentration, peace, harmony, insight and mindfulness. Some practices are old as Buddhism itself while some are new, recently developed by the modern practitioners.

One of the oldest is found in the Noble Eightfold Path itself called right mindfulness. In this type of meditation, complete focus is given on the four foundations: your body, your feelings, your mind and the content of your mind. Under this holistic meditative practice, two very important events can be experienced. First is tranquility, the state of complete concentration which can pave the way for increased awareness. Second is insight, this is the set of tools you need to discern the truth beyond the false realities.

Here are some meditative practices that you can do:

http://dharmawisdom.org/teachings/articles/starting-mindfulness-meditation-practice

http://www.tm.org/meditation-techniques

John Baskin

http://www.how-to-meditate.org

http://liveanddare.com/types-of-meditation/

Chapter 6: Festivals

Part of being a practicing Buddhist is the celebration of important days in a year. Each of these festivals commemorates a certain event in the life of the Buddha or is meant to highlight a specific teaching. It is also a time to congregate with other believers and reaffirm your community with them.

New Year (January, February or April)

This is celebrated in different days depending on the location where you are or which Buddhist school you follow. For example, in Asian countries, the Buddhist New Year starts on April, 3 days after the first full moon. This is the Theravadin date for celebration. For the Mahayana celebration, the New Year starts in the first full moon on January. Celebrating this day often involves

Magha Puha (March)

The first full moon of March is meant to commemorate a vital event in the human life of the Buddha. According to tradition, during this day, the Buddha was said to have traveled to a city to meet with 1,250 of the most enlightened saints, Arahats. They were his disciples and met him to pay their respects. It is a day worth celebrating because it shows an important miracle. No call was made for the meeting but all 1,250 came at their own accord. Celebrating this day often involves the abstinence from committing any sin, ritual purifications and performs good deeds.

Vesak (May)

This is one of the most important days for the Buddhist calendar. This celebrates more than the birthday of Buddha but also his death and his enlightenment. It occurs in the first full moon of May. The event involves contemplation of Buddha's teachings. Often, people will hear or perform longer recitations of important sutras. Meat is also avoided and white is worn.

Asalha Puja (July)

Celebrated on the first moon of July, this festivity is meant to remind Buddhist of the day when Buddha transmitted his first teaching, the wheel of Dhamma. This first teaching is given importance becaues all future teachings given by the Buddha revolves around the foundation set by this first teaching. To celebrate, Buddhists will go to temples, offer gifts and listen to teachings given by the monks.

Uposatha (monthly)

These are specific days in a given month that occur in the phases of the moon. Most Buddhists fast during this festivity. Longer sutras are recited, temples are visited, meditations are done and more conscious decisions to do good deeds and avoid evil are done during these days. When a person is unable to visit a temple, he can commemorate this event by doing good deeds in his immediate vicinity, such as giving food to the needy.

Songkran (April)

This is a Buddhist festivity celebrated by Thais. During this festivity, there is a ritual cleansing of houses and clothes to symbolize purification. People will also shower monks with gives such as perfumed water.

Loy Krathong (November)

To commemorate the footprints of the Buddha that left their mark on an Indian river, this festival is also done in rivers. People will bring bowls made of leaves and fill them with flowers, candles or incense and release them in the water. The bowls will then float and create lighted prints in the water.

John Baskin

Chapter 7: Modern Day Buddhism

Worldwide Network

There is an estimated 350 million Buddhist across the world, representing around 6% of total world population. Thailand has the largest proportion but China has the largest population of Buddhists, numbering to more than 100 million. When it is clustered together with other world religions, it is the fifth in rank.

While there is no governing body that centralized control, like the Pope and Vatican for Roman Catholicism, Buddhism is interconnected by a network of temples, represented by gurus and students. Expansion of Buddhism from the East to the West is the result of several factors. It can be due to Westerners either going to the Eastern countries to study and return to their home country to create centers of their own or gurus are invited to travel to the West and teach in a foreign land as missionaries.

Below are some online resources that you can use as reference to locate Buddhist temples or centers. These sites are also filled with articles and videos of teachings made by gurus. Buddhism may be an old belief system but its practitioners have used the power of technology to bridge the physical gaps and barriers made by geography.

http://www.buddhanet.net

http://www.diamondway-buddhism.org

http://www.thebuddhism.net

http://www.buddhanet.info/wbd/

http://shambhala.org

http://www.everydayzen.org/index.php?option=com_teaching &Itemid=26

http://www.buddhanet.info/wbd/country.php?country_id=2

http://buddhistchurchesofamerica.org

Remember to conduct due diligence and perform skepticism when visiting the above links or visiting the temples and centers listed. Though you can gain important teachings from a guru Buddhism is a personal path and journey. There is no rule that orders you to attend temple services, however you can greatly benefit from the teachings as transmitted to your by teachers.

Famous Buddhists

While the Eastern expansion of Buddhism can be traced to a network of gurus and lamas who taught ordinary citizens all the way to kings and emperors of the ancient world, the Western expansion can be traced from different sources. Migrants from the East to the West brought with them their practices and meditation were done in the privacy of the temples or their homes. However, the increased interest on Buddhism, especially in the Western countries, was due to the upper classes of European and American countries.

For example, members of the nobility and aristocracy were very curious of anything Asian and exotic, which included Buddhism. As part of an exhibition, they will regularly invite a guru and sponsor their trip to their manors as a spectacle. Overtime, Buddhism firmly planted its roots in society. Today, some of the best spokespersons of Buddhism are no longer the upper class or the gurus themselves but personalities who have found the beliefs to match their personal convictions.

In America, Hollywood celebrities have given Buddhism the spotlight. Jennifer Aniston, Orlando Bloom, Kate Bosworth, Jeff Bridges, Penelope Cruz, Richard Gere, Kate Hudson, Angelina Jolie, Miranda Kerr, Jennifer Lopez, Alanis Morissette, Keannu Reeves, Sarah Jessica Parker, Brad Pitt, Sting, Tina Turner, Uma Thurman and Naomi Watts are few of Hollywoods' A-listers who are known to be practicing Buddhists. Athletes such as Robert Baggio, Phil Jackson, Alex Rodriguez and Tiger Woods are also Buddhists. Industry giants, Elaine and Steve Wynn, William Ford and Steve Jobs are also Buddhists. Bill Clinton is also said to be a Buddhist.

Gurus, Lamas & the Dalai Lama

As there are famous Buddhist celebrities and personalities, there are also key figures and authorities in Buddhism, they are the teachers, known by many names and honorifics such as gurus and lamas. Some of those viewed as authorities in the beliefs are:

Sakyong Mipham Rinpoche

Ani Pema Chodron

Sharon Salzberg

Joan Halifax Roshi

Reggie Ray

Robert Thurman

Judith Simmer-Brown

Thich Nhat Hanh

Khenpo Tsultrim Gyamtso Rinpoche

Her Eminence, Karmapa Khandro Rinpoche

His Holiness, the 14th Dalai Lama Tenzin Gyatso

Again, remember to conduct your due diligence and practice skepticism in evaluating the teachers that you choose for your path. It does not mean that the teacher you are considering is not included in the above list means that he or she is not qualified. In fact, some of the teachers in the list are quite inaccessible in ordinary means, because some prefer a live of quiet contemplation. However, there are those that are not in this list that are accessible but have been declared as giving false teachings. Be mindful when choosing your guide or teacher and refer to the foundations of the school or tradition of your choice in evaluating the guru's authenticity.

Regardless of the school or the tradition that you choose, the principles, doctrines and teachings listed in this book is merely the tip of the iceberg. As you go deeper into your study of Buddhism and as you practice it in your daily life, you will gain something that no book can ever provide, which is insight.

Only in the experience of Buddhism can insight be truly gained. However, the purpose of this book is to give you a solid foundation or a comprehensive first step towards the understanding of Buddhism, not as a religion but as entire way of life. When you have the information gained from this book, you are primed toward the second step of your journey and that is experiencing the life of a Buddhist.

Application does not have to be mysterious or esoteric; it does not often require incense burning or ritual robes being worn. From doing your own set of meditative practices, visiting a temple to recite or hear sutras to giving help to the needy and the suffering, these are all practical applications of the path taught by Buddha, regardless of how simple or how grand a scale that you will do it.

In this life, it will not always be harmony or tranquility; there will be periods of difficulty and challenges. Know that this is natural and part of the journey itself; however you must also know that these sufferings are also impermanent. The more you practice Buddhism that more that you will begin to see for people, things and your realm for exactly what they are. You will clear your eyes from illusions or falsehoods that only blur reality and cloud your journey. When the path is clear, you will have a broken one link in the chain of samsara and a glimpse of the infinite.

I hope that you are able to find more value in your life through the information resonating inside this book. I do my best to provide content that is accurate, uplifting, and valuable to the reader. If you have any constructive feedback that you would like to offer, or feel like the content in my book can be improved in any way, please feel free to contact me at:

faithinknowledge@bookenthuziast.com

If you happened to find value in this book, I have a favor to ask of you. Do you have the time to leave an honest review for this book on Amazon? As someone wanting to take my life and others to greater heights, I'd really appreciate if you can spread the word by leaving an honest review ☺

★☆★FREE BONUS SECTION★☆★

Zen: Tranquil Quotes, Tips, and Short Meditations Using Zen Buddhism

Day 1: What is Zen?

The ancients found that thoughts are powerful things--good thoughts and bad are equally potent, they learned. Some of them were persistently curious enough to learn that when they re-positioned their thoughts, they could eliminate physical, as well as mental, intrusion with a little practice. They began to devote themselves to a system of meditation that cleared their thinking of everything. When they recognized the beneficial results, they gave their practice a name. They called it "Zen," meaning "absorption" or "meditative state."

Quote for the Day:

"Empty your mind of everything. Let the mind become still," says Lao Tzu, author of the Tao Te Ching. (600 B. C. E.)

Tranquil Tip of the Day:

Now you are ready to experience your first lesson: Listen. Then listen for nothing.

A new way of sitting . . .

Learning to meditate is the first step in achieving *tranquility*. Being receptive begins with putting your body into a posture that allows your mind the freedom it needs to rest, settle, and be calm. Sitting with your back straight, keep your head up; imagine your head is above the trees and breathe deeply, slowly and silently counting your breaths until you reach 100. Try not to fall asleep; calmness is the goal.

Day 2: Enlightenment

So, this is exciting. On the second day, already you have a brief idea of what Zen is and today you're learning about Buddha "enlightenment" or "awakening" as the traditional legend has it. Concerning its first practitioner, Siddhartha Gautama (who was called a "sage" and subsequently became the Buddha), and lived in eastern India. It is estimated he lived between the sixth and fourth centuries, B. C. E.

"Buddha" eventually becomes "Buddhism."

At this time, the object of learning to meditate is to become Buddha or "awakened through enlightenment." Becoming Buddha is not a sometime thing. It is accomplished through consistent, devotional activity, so it is important that it be pursued every day.

Quote for the Day:

"Knowing constancy is insight. Knowing constancy, the mind is open."
- Lao Tzu

Tranquil Tip of the Day:

Find room in your life to practice your meditation for at least 20 minutes a day. Whether you start your day with it, or do it before retiring at bedtime, being *constant* will give Zen a fair opportunity to work its way into your life.

For now, find a time and stick to it for a few days. You can always change it. Buddhism doesn't mean "rigid" or "imposing," so choose your best time and light a candle to help you frame these moments as a reward in your day. Be seated with your excellent posture, head up and counting breaths.

And remember that a calm mind generates the clarity to take a next step:

"You should sit in meditation for twenty minutes every day—unless you're too busy; then you should sit for an hour."
- Zen Proverb

For more information, go to: http://amzn.to/1Kx8tV8

John Baskin

About the Author

Hi fellow reader,

My name is John Baskin and I am a student of life and love, seeing the world as one great experiment. I've lived a large portion of my life making decisions based on the opinions of others, which led to discontent and bitterness because I wasn't living in line with what truly resonates with me and, though people around me may not have been able to see that, the truth was revealed during moments of solitude.

I picked up journaling during my latter years in college and it became a ritual for me to record anything that came to mind. Though I was never an exceptional student of English during my academic years, I see writing as a way to express myself and it's been very therapeutic for me. I love the concept of journaling because it allows me to put all of my thoughts down and then look at them from an outsider's perspective, which allows me to identify patterns of thinking that are either empowering or disempowering the way I live. It is journaling that fuels my writing and I believe that a life worth living is worth recording.

As a fan of psychology and the personal development arena, I have a passion for creating deep connections, understanding people's mentalities as best I can, and fostering the environment for them to discover the personal power they possess to transform their life and live with a surge of enthusiasm and fulfillment. My hope is that this energy will be conveyed in my writing.

For you to pick up one of my books, I take it to mean that you are interested in improving your standard of living, and I have great respect for someone who is committed to personal growth and strengthening that desire in others.

Cheers to your path to ever-expanding greatness,

John Baskin

PS: I do my best to provide content that is *accurate*, *uplifting*, and *valuable* to the reader. If you have any <u>constructive feedback</u> that you would like to offer, or feel like the content in my book can be <u>improved</u> in any way, please feel free to contact me at:

<u>faithinknowledge@bookenthuziast.com</u>

Manufactured by Amazon.ca
Bolton, ON